This Notebook Belongs To

____

Printed in the USA
CPSIA information can be obtained
at www.ICGtesting.com
LVHW062139290823
756687LV00041B/1117

9 781070 996066